WONDERMAN'S POETRY

Poems of Pain
Maybe of Hope
Someday

By

Wonderman37

PublishAmerica
Baltimore

First printing

ISBN: 1-4137-4989-5
PUBLISHED BY PUBLISHAMERICA, LLLP
www.publishamerica.com
Baltimore

Printed in the United States of America

[Untitled]

Though the voids of emptiness extended.
Hollow feelings, shadows
whispering thru their nightly visits.
Running scared, nowhere to hide
From the demons of my past; they still come.
Still caged I am, like a wild beast that I feel like.
To mock me in my time of need, I run away.
The hell that my tormented life has become.
Still I really do try with all of my heart to change.
With no hope of surviving much longer, I run.
With no hope, no chance,
no prayer for my saddened soul.
So as always, out of desperation, I run again.
But at this moment I realized
that my options empty out.
Still no other choice except to run away once again.

MY OWN WORLD

All alone in this world of my own making.
No one is there to hurt me
or to help me either.
No one there to despise, hate,
or even to love me.
No one there to beat, abuse, rob,
or even to love me.
No one there to run me down,
or even to give me praises.
Yes, no one there, but my body, heart, and soul.
No negative feelings on this here planet.
But then again no one here
to make my life worth living either.

[UNTITLED]

He looked older,than his true age.
Wild, wavy, hair made him look mad.
His eyes were as black as the darkest coals.
Maybe, his heart wasn't evil deep inside.
But his appearance made him look that way.
But it was never my call to judge him in the first place.
Besides, you have to look deeper beyond the outside.
Forget it all; then look deeper into their soul.
While having an open mind to other people.
Only then shall you see the true human being.
Still the judgment rights should only be given to the lord.

FRESH WOUNDS

Another tear, another fresh wound.
Another torn hole in my painful heart.
It appears to me the thing I crave the most.
The love is to be denied from me forever.
Been looking, searching for her a life to appear.
But searching in vain is the feeling that I am getting.
'Cause I am being kept from finding her.
Don't even know if she is still alive now.
All I know is I need to find her soon, very soon.
Still my stallion flies down every roadside.
She must be out there somewhere under the same sky.
Still I shall never give up on my search for her.
Just wish the heavens above would show me her location.
Soon our hearts shall be one, united forever I hope.
Then we both shall thank god for the wonderful miracle.

Half Full, Half Empty

The empty part of the glass represents.
All the uncultivable goals that I set for myself.
All of the hopes that I dreamt of my entire life.
The valuables that I gained then lost again.
The women who confess to be my miss right.
But then show me the hellish side of my heaven.
All of the torment and sorrow
dwelling in the darkest part of my soul.
All the beauty seen by someone else eyes.
The full part of the half empty glass represents.
All of the dreams that are still accomplishable.
Knowing deep in my burdened heart
I am still heavenbound.
Seeing despite all the pain
I felt that I still held tight to my morals.
All the pain, misery, and torment
that made me a stronger man.
All of the love inside of me
that still could belong to my miss right.
All of the experiences
that I could share with other people.
Finally a future that is still up for grabs in this life.

[Untitled]

One life, two souls sharing.
Just one purpose, two hearts entwine.
One world, two people sharing the love there.
One mind, two brains in tune with each other.
Love brought them here, to nurture their love.
Faith in each other, kept the love growing.
Only through death and hell shall their love.
Be twisted and lost for all times to come.
The darkness shall fall upon them.
But with the help of the father up above.
The light shall cast a healing coat upon them.
Keeping them as one, throughout all time.
Staying together forever as one for all of eternality.
A love that is stronger than any steel here on earth.
With this love, they shall remain invincible

SHE WAS

She was the sparkling light of my life.
She was the heaven, that I been searching for.
She was the reason that kept me breathing.
She was the deserted island that rescues me.
Now and forever she is the destiny I was born to.
But still after all this time, I am still all alone.
Waiting for my beautiful queen to rescue me.
Still waiting to fulfill the wondrous prophecy.
Then she and I shall become one, sharing our life.
Being together, with such a strong love together.
She was and will always forever be
the queen of my heart.
'Till we meet though, I am merely an empty glass
waiting to be filled.
Of the sweet nectar people call red wine.
Then she and I will forever stand as one.

BEST OF TIMES

Even during the best of all times.
The worst of all times ever recorded.
There is no comparison to what your heart said to mine.
It was the sweetest of times, when we were together.
When I truly believed that you really loved me.
Still etched in my mind in all of it infamously
When you begged me to just walk away from us.
Showed me that maybe, you never loved me at all.
As the tears began to flood across my eyes.
Confusion ran wild and deep inside of my mind.
Forever trying to avoid the obliviousness of the situation.
That the something missing was coming from you.
Maybe, the love was never there to begin with.

THE DARKNESS

I felt the darkness, deep inside of me.
It overwhelms me at times.
Mine isn't a evil mind of fog and darkness.
It merely shows my saddened soul
Raining deep inside as my options fade.
Helplessness dwells deep inside,
Feeling like I have no reason to live at times,
Like I am just barely surviving in life.
Not even living at times, just surviving.
Each day the fog of emptiness expands to higher heights.
They soar; all of my hopes are fading fast.
Left by the fog of torment, still I struggle to escape this fog
That becomes worse the more I struggle to survive.
As I've searched for that special feeling,
I've gone from one roadblock to the next,
Searching for that very special lady,
Hoping that she would turn my life all sunny and light.
She would give me a real reason
to want to wake up every morning,
Just so I could stare at her beautiful smiling face again.
But all of the cards seemed stacked against me.
Searching hard, only to remain empty handed of love,
Still my heart refuses to give up on the search
To the pain of my wounded heart.
My soul dies a little every night.
I shall always search for her, 'til I find her.

WONDROUS WORLD

As I stood there watching in wonder.
At the wondrous sight of beauty.
As the sun began to rise once more.
Things like that I find so very beautiful.
The most glorious ones are free.
Now that I am homeless and all alone.
I see a different side to this wondrous world of ours.
That we all live then die in.
Being a sensitive romantic.
I find real pleasure in all of god's creations.
Thank you god for the gifts, you gave us all.
To give us all hopes in our times of need.
And yet you keep your eyes on us all.

My Father

Still after all of these years.
My dad died, almost twenty years ago.
Still struggling to prove my worth to him.
Still falling short, in showing him.
That I am worthy in carrying on the family name.
Still struggling to get back on my feet too.
Yet every time I get close to getting my life back.
I slip and fall back into the gutter of hell.
To have to start all over once again.
A daily struggle to survive in this uncaring world today.
With no rewards in the very end.
Just trying to make my father proud of me.
He was the best dad ever.
He was always there and watching out for me.

Heaven Bound

Heavenbound is where I stand right now
My life here on Earth is nothing.
But a doorway to the Heavens themselves.
Still the struggles here are many in this life.
But someday soon, peace shall reign in me.
But 'til that day appears the suffering is for real.
Right now my hardships and tests are a daily event.
All I need to do though is endure this mortal pain.
'Cause soon I will be home for the rest of eternally
Still god is watching out for my sadden soul.
Cause he truly does love all his children.
And he keeps a watchful eye upon each of us.
He suffers with us in all of our worst of times.
So I am trying to be strong in all of my times of needs,
Even during all of my daily struggles.

DIFFERENT LIVES

One night, two lives changed forever.
One life, two souls touched one another.
Two hearts combine into one single life.
One dream big enough for two to share together.
He loves her more than his life is worth to him.
Two caring people united through out all times.
This child has the best of both of them in him.
They love him with a strong, unconditional love.
When you find this special kind of love in your life.
You can honestly say that
you been blessed, truly blessed.
'Cause love is the greatest of all miracles ever to happen.
That only a chosen few get to grasp in their life.

TORMENTED LOST SOUL

Warm-hearted, saddened soul deep inside.
Tormented soul full of emptiness inside.
Used and discarded by so many people.
But still alive, wishing it was otherwise.
So very much heartache, just in one life.
Still I continue to survive to find my special place.
In this cold and cruel world that we all live in.
Only god truly loves us all here
on this planet called heart.
As I finally realize deep down in my aching heart.
So now I begin to pray to god for some inner peace.
Feeling at my very lowest
in this sad, bitter life of mine.
Still I press to move forward
in this painful road to inner destruction.

Doom and Destruction

Doom and destruction fills the darken air.
As the sadness engulfing the aching souls.
She struggle to grasp an invisible prize.
All of her worldly possessions are at her fingertips.
Still the emptiness deep inside of her feels very hollow.
His world was colliding with self destruction.
His marriage ended leaving him, very empty-handed.
Even his great paying job was gone,
leaving him broken down.
Now all that he was left with was miserable memories.
Of all the glory that was once held in his mind's eye.
Together they start a new beginning
in their wonderful life.
With the worst of their nightmares in their past.

EMPTINESS INSIDE

Standing along the roadside of life.
Wondering where to go from here.
Tired of the entire emotional tornado.
Twisting my heart and soul into a warped hell.
Still evading the questions
that I already have the answers to.
Yet the pain keeps my heart in a hellish prison.
After it threw away the key, where, I haven't a clue.
I keep sinking in the quicksands of misfortune.
And a sadness that forever twists my inner soul.
Only Heaven bound shall put a true smile upon my face.
Til that time arrives my title here on earth will be foolish.
The court jester, clown the foolish pride I wield.

Heroes Of The Bravely Kind

This poem can never truly say how lucky we truly are.
The soldiers, police officers, firemen, and sheriffs.
Who risk their lives every day for us people?
Without their heroics, in time of our greatest needs.
We would never know the level of sacrifices.
Laying their lives and families' life on the line for us.
'Cause it affects their friends and families
if something was to happen to them.
This loss is greater than even the loss
of a sports personality.
Or even a famous writer or actor could affect us.
'Cause these people are the rarest of kind,
brave heroes.
Who, going to work every day, knows that it could
easily be their last?
I just hope that this world appreciates what they do for us.

DREAM SMASHED

Another dream smashed along the side of the road.
Leaving me once again with nothing to my name.
It is always the way things turn out for me.
I guess I am lucky because I am not a materialistic male.
'Cause then I would be even more depressed.
Then what I am already, Lord Jesus.
Another night in this world all alone still.
Struggling to get my life straightened out still.
It had been a long three years for me, since I had a life.
My life has never been fully happy one,
not even in my married years.
More secure maybe,
but still not what you would call happy.
So much has been taken from me,
that I could still shed tears over.
Looking toward the great Heavens
for some support from god.
But still no answers do I get
in this life I dwell in now.

Tormented Life Of Hell

The demons that dwell in my life are hellish.
I did the best that I could to go to heaven when I die.
But the monsters that tear at my heart and soul.
Torment me restlessly, trying to destroy my life.
Still the lord father in heaven, test me still.
Hopefully after all is said and done in the end.
I still am going to the great Heavens above.
All of my life I been searching for a reason to live.
Never truly finding one that makes me happy.
I am really looking forward to seeing the Heavens' gates.
The search is still on in my saddened soul,
a reason to move on.
In this bittersweet life that I have made
more into a torture chamber.

Lightning Strikes Twice

When the lightning struck my life,
It shined like an eerie gloomy ray
Of sorrow and darkness would, full of despair.
The light shall always be seen in my mind,
Reminding me how easily we can fall from grace.
So once things change in my bitter, saddened life,
All the experiences that made my world crumble
Remind me that I need to clean them out of my mind
So that maybe I can for once move forward in this life.
Even the pains, guilt, sorrow, and feelings
I had as a wee child, are opened up
For me to somehow make some ammends
to this awful feeling.
That has never been properly cleaned out
then disposed of.
With only the help from god way above,
can I move forward?
Then and only then, maybe,
I will become a better man.

COLD WIND BREWING

The cold wind is coming on strong.
Still feeling the ice, even in my deepest regions.
At the core of my saddened soul and even in my heart.
Praying, Lord Jesus help me to make it to the next level.
Wishing hard for God to bring me to the Heavenly gates.
Guess my prayers are not going to be answered now.
Still moving on in this life without a prayer to survive.
Never really succeeding at anything in this life,
Becoming nothing more than a joke to other people.
Just existing in a life of a tormented fool.
Ready to give people something to poke fun and laugh at.
At the idiot that I have become of lately.

Twisted Lies

Twisted lies and a tormented life.
Demented dreams of a dreaded, doomed.
Satan, prince of pain laughing at my ill gains.
Trying to refuel the suffering that made me sad.
Still the ragged only get worst when I begin to think.
Driving me further on the road to self-destruction.
My soul is soaked from the sweat of nervousness.
Still trying to hang onto the values I hold close.
Innocents lost to the helplessness of the darkness.
That binds my heart and soul to this earthly hell.
With the memories, the past dragging my world deeper
Into the oblivion of ill-fated death and destruction.

MISERY

Torment, pain, misery, and hell.
Doomed to suffer like this 'till death appears.
To stay forever in the darkness of torment.
Still struggling to recapture a life that seems lost to me.
At one time, a life time ago,
I held a better position in this life.
But taking it for granted cost me dearly,
now comesthe penalty.
For the mistakes that I have made hold me prisoner.
Showing me what truly happens
to foolish, prideful people.
So here I stand now,
at the cross-road I am destined to cross.
With the lost memories
that still surge through my aching brain.
The values that I still hold onto in this losing battle life.
Thinking that with a strong love,
nothing else could hurt you.
Was I ever wrong?
The love, first off, was not really that strong.
Secondly, I lost everything
due to my short-sighted mind.

[UNTITLED]

I was lost. Looking for some escape.
But a friend and his wife kept me straight.
I might have been dead elsewhere.
If I hadn't had them as close friends.
Time might come when we argue a lot
But still they have been there for me.
Even the times I have left Iowa completely.

BEST AND WORST

Even the best of moments
and the worst of times don't compare
to what your heart once said to mine.
It was the sweetest of times
when I truly thought you really did love me.
Still remembering the darkest of nights
when you begged me to pack up and leave.
Confused deep inside, that just maybe
you may have never actually loved me.
As the tears flowed down my eyes
the night I walked out of your life forever.
Still trying to avoid the facts, before my eyes still.
That I lost everything over a lost battle.
Trying to find that missing something
that deeply was never there in first place.
Still here I stand dazed and confused, wondering.

Forever Friends

The Bierman family helped me to say afloat.
Staying rooted long enough to begin again.
A new life still struggling and fears
made me want to run away from a fading life.
Still they kept supporting me with words and money.
At times telling me my life has to get better eventually.
Many times I wanted to give up and fade into nothingness.
Feeling the pressure from many other people.
I stayed and faced my inner demons.
My life at times seems to be getting a little better.
and slowly I am trying to get a normal life back once more.
Thank god for friends like them.
Still I feel like I am living in hell if not for them.
Still I stuggle from time to time.
But now I have new goals to meet to better myself.

LIGHTNING

When lightning struck my life
it shined a darkened, gloomy ray
of sorrow and darkened despair.
The light will always remind me of my life
'cause of the experiences it brought.
Now that it has consumed my entire being
it reminds me of the sorrow
that was always a major source.
Throughout my entire life, even as a youngster.
the awareness, now that I know
it was locked away before.
Deep inside the realm of my inner thoughts
only to be released at that moment.
Today, I guess my mind was finally opened
the only solution I have now
is to learn to control the emotions.

Good Luck, Bad Luck

His heart was as big as the outdoors,
His soul as pure as new-fallen snow.
His honesty was very true, too.
He was close to being a saint.
But his luck was very bad too.
When it came to the heart
women that he had fallen for
all played him like a violin.
Still he searched for the love
that he desperately craved.
Still he kept searching for her
that one, very special lady.
That would rescue him from the loneliness.
Still he searched for the true kind of love.
Struggling to find her was rough
Still in his heart, he never gaved up.

TROUBLED WATERS

The troubled waters of my life
were darkened with pain and misery
Stormy weather always filled
my blackened nights with rage.
The furies of the sotrm
knew the saddness had no end.
Just when I thought I saw
a beautiful rainbow ahead,
suddenly another storm arose
to forever keep away the calm of happiness.
Still I tried to escape the struggles
only to keep losing the battles.
Maybe someday a true rainbow shall appear.
One that will not vanish so fast,
Finally giving me a little peace for a change.

She Is

She is the light of my life.
She is the heaven I was breathing.
She is the deserted island that rescues me.
Now and forever, she is mydestiny.
After all this time, I still stand alone
waiting to fill her and my prophecy
of becoming one, sharing our lives together.
Being together 'til the end tears us apart.
I'm her knight, waiting to rescue her.
She is my queen waiting to share her soul with me.
'Til we meet, I will be but an empty glass
waiting to be filled with the sweet wine.
Biding my time, waiting for true love to arrive.

MONKEY

Many demons in my life left me chained
to the darkenss and pain that dwelt in my life.
Searching for a little bit of sunshine
only to end up struggling with the
monkeys or demons that keep me down.
Feelings of loneliness and sorrow
keep me losing the goals in my life.
Slowly, I am trying to stand up once more
but they still attempt to push me back.
Only when they are exorcised, from the demons
will I be able to stand up proudly again.
Today, though I think I might be
little bit stronger then yesterday.
Seeking help to overcome them
was a struggle in itself.
Still I am working harder now.

CONSUMED

Consumed by a hunger that wells deep inside
my soul is filled with mystic pain.
The pain seems not normal to me
it just keeps me down in the darkest
of hells that I never could imagine.
Still I try with all my might
to overcome the hurdles in my way.
Struggling to keep the pace I've been going
hoping to put it out of my mind and win
this battle that is ahead of me here.
With a mighty sword I swing as I drive on
to conquer the darkness laid before me
Looking toward God for the support
that I crave to win this battle ahead.
Once the victory is mine then I can rest.

[UNTITLED]

As the winds blew over there
The memories of her still waited there.
For the torment that it kept up.
Wiser wisher, I was, but the truth still stands.
the emptiness still rages deep in my heart.
For her, my heart still rings true.
'Til my dying breath breathes nomore.
Here I shall stand, loving her— my angel.
Even if she will never know 'tis true.
My heart will always cry out for her.
the queen of my darkest memories.
Will always haunt the deepest bowels of my heart.

PAINFUL REALITIES

Through the darkness I wonder.
Sensing the void of pain in my life.
That just will never vanish from my life.
Hearing the evil voice ringing through my ears.
Still alive but truely wanting to die.
But this life holds me as it prisioner.
In a grizzly grip the heartache still exists.
Forever to hide inside the darkest reaches.
Of the forbidden zone, of the soul inside of me.
That twitches with pain, even in bliss.
The hurt will not sustain inside of me

Time Lost

In my life I felt so very lost.
The lost time, when my life could be better.
Like the lost love that was never to be real.
Or the lost soul that I felt like I was so much.
Still at times I wonder why I was so important.
To this wonderful savior that reigns above.
Still today was it worth it to him to have kept me safe.
Especially in the darkest hours of my dark life.
The answers never come—why did you pick me god?
When there were people who could offer this world more.
Who died a fruitless life,
with a soul purer than mine ever was.
Yet...the answers still never come; only the lord knows.

NOTHING WITHOUT YOU

I know that we are over forever now.
But I feel the nothing, still inside of me.
Since you asked me to leave your life forever.
My life has lost all signs of direction now.
I am feeling the pain ofnothing, deep inside of me.
I know that I should be moving on with my life now.
But how can I, when my life is nothing without you.
What would I be moving onto, now that I lost you?
At this very moment in my life, all is lost inside.
Nothing but memories of us remain, deep inside.
I heard that my broken heart will eventually heal.
How can it when my heart has been shattered now.
All the nothinginess deep inside can never be heal.
I still wish I could be holding you in my arms tonight.

FORGOTTEN

Deep inside of my inner core
Dwells the memories of my forgotten woes.
Still I am moving on to even darker lores.
Struggling through all of the emptiness inside.
Forgotten lies that I have been telling myself.
Still on this cold darkened day,I still stand alone.
In the hollow area of my saddened sou-emptiness.
Moving on to what, I will never know for sure.
'Cause all seems lost in this bitter, cold life of mine.
So please, Father God, grant me some kind of refuge
From this hollow prison that I dwell in tonight.
Maybe even a little peace of mind, I doubt now.
Waiting for the darkness to arrive and no more will I be.

TREASURES

In my life the bitterness unfolds darkness.
Not sure what is exactly hidden from my emotional mind.
Still, I am searching for something that must be missing
From this empty life of mine, and praying to my father
Who lives way above, in the heavenly skies
To answer my prays, then maybe, shed some light
On the all meaningful purpose that guilds my life.
I need an answer because this hollow feeling is too dark.
So I stare deep inside of my psyche for some inner meaning.
But still, I come up always empty-handed.
All of my memories have hidden important information
That might show me why I was put on this very earth.

Unbreakable Sprit

Even in my darkest hours here on earth,
I always seem to struggle with everything I do.
Even at an early age, the problems seemed many.
Still I stand all alone, yet I still am existing on Earth.
I may complain many times, yet I am still here.
Seems the more that I seem to suffer here on earth,
The stronger that I become, but it is the truth.
Whether I like it or not, I have to accept it.
No matter how much I complain,
it not going to do any good.
I'm guessing all I can do is accept the fate
that my heavenly father gave me,
And use it to glorify his heavenly name
by doing what is right,
Thanking him too, for giving me this much honor
by using me for his purpose.

Rainbows and Blues

God created rain to make us sad and to make us cry,
To cleanse our eyes of dirt and other particles in the air.
He also wanted to cleanse our hearts of painful things.
Then finally, he wanted to show us true beauty.
So then god made rainbows and sunrises to lift our spirits.
Make us all smile, and then be joyful once again.
He loves us all so very much, that he created love.
He also wanted all of us to be able to dream
in our hour of need.
That is the main reason that he has created
the beautiful rainbows.
In the darkest hour of our life comes a storm brewing.
Then it leaves without a clue of why,
 leaving a rainbow of joy.
So remember this anytime you see a rainbow
in your weary life.
It is a promise from our heavenly father,
of a new beginning.

Love Lost Twice

In our saddened lives here on this earth,
We all go through many changes, losing the love,
At times, of someone so very special to us.
Still, we must move forward all alone, without the,.
Looking at a future of pain, loneliness, and suffering.
Still our heavenly father is up there looking down,
Ready to send us a angel in our darkest of times,
Wanting to protect us, even from ourselves.
We move on in this life with a heart full of loneliness,
struggling to get back on track of this life we live,
Looking toward the heavens for some comfort in life.
From this awful, horrible storm that has hit us hard,
Still our heavenly father has not deserted us.

TRAIN OF PAIN

We choose to board this train without thought,
Not even realizing the pain that is involved..
So then, without reason, the pain becomes visible.
But we notice it too late to jump off of it.
So we ride 'til it ends up stopping, but it is too late
to save us from the unbearable pain that hits us.
Struggling to stop the train seems too hard for us.
Then we somehow figure out that demons from hell
are the conducters of this train
 that we jumped on by mistake.
Then we pray to god to take away all of our pain
And heal us all from the temptation that Satan gave us.
But god can only save us when we are ready to be saved.

MANY LIVES LEFT

In my life I felt like I was a cat,
Living even though I should really be dead.
Still, there must be some reason for me to still be here.
Only God knows the true reason that he kept me here.
I guess it is not my call, whether I live or not,
Because for some reason that I am unaware of,
I am part of his master plan.
Maybe I am meant to be a missionary
for my heavenly father, without knowing it.
All that I know is that my purpose has not
been fulfilled yet.
Only when that happens,
will I be able to go to my home in heaven.
'Til that time does arrive, my place will be here,
doing I do not know what.
All that I know is that when my times does come,
I will be ready for it.
'Til that time,
you can meet me anytime you like on this earth.

LITTLE THINGS

Little things, like memories
or loving arms wrapped around you
Are the most precious things that we can get
here on earth.
Friends that truly do care or families that really love us,
Or wonderful memories
that have been made from love,
Or pictures of our children doing the sweetest of things—
Those are things that make life
worth living every day.
Happiness, in the purest of forms, are made of this too,
Or crying a million tears of joy
and wondering about these special things.
Having such a wonderful savior in our life—
that is the most important thing
In this entire life of ours—
The only reason that we need to live.
A beautiful wife, who loves you and even adores you
is a little thing.
That makes life worth living here on this earth.

Innocence Shattered

He was once a loving child, full of love.
The dreams that he has dreamt were wonderful too:
Dreams of helping the weak and even the downtrodden.
He cried when he saw others sad or hurt.
He was so full of love and compassion in his heart,
But that was before the innocence was shattered.
Now he is a twisted mess of love and loneliness,
full of sorrow.
His strengths, at one time,
were the weakness that he has now.
This young, little boy that innocence has shattered,
Was once a very caring young boy, who still has a heart
That is full of love and one day may be full of joy,
but he was sad now.
Already, he was ready to give up on the innocence
that he once held tightly.

Dreams

When you think of dreams,
    remember me.
When you feel surrounded by love,
    remember me.
When the tears flow so freely,
    remember me.
When your heart starts to beat faster,
    remember me.
When you grow old and still are very proud,
    remember me.
When you think about the past that you lived,
    remember me.
When your hair is all gray and you are ready to move on,
    remember me.
Remember me 'cause I will still be here for you
    in all of my dreams.
My love for you, for us, will never turn cold.
Mine heart will always be yours for the taking,
    any time or any place.
Just think of me any time, cause my love for you
    will only grow stronger.
No matter where or what,
    just remember me from time to time.